Read-About® Holidays

Ramadan

By David F. Marx

Consultants
Nanci R. Vargus, Ed.D.
Primary Multiage Teacher
Decatur Township Schools, Indianapolis, Indiana

Katharine A. Kane, Reading Specialist
Former Language Arts Coordinator,
San Diego County Office of Education

Children's Press®
A Division of Scholastic Inc.
New York   Toronto   London   Auckland   Sydney
Mexico City   New Delhi   Hong Kong
Danbury, Connecticut

Designer: Herman Adler Design
Photo Researcher: Caroline Anderson
The photo on the cover shows a Muslim child praying.

Library of Congress Cataloging-in-Publication Data

Marx, David F.
    Ramadan / by David F. Marx; consultants, Nanci R. Vargus,
Katharine A. Kane.
        p. cm. — (Rookie read-about holidays)
    Includes index.
    Summary: A simple introduction to the traditions and festivities of the
Muslim holiday, Ramadan.
    ISBN 0-516-22269-4 (lib. bdg.)   0-516-27377-9 (pbk.)
    1. Ramadan—Juvenile literature. [1. Ramadan. 2. Fasts and feasts—
Islam. 3. Islam—Customs and practices. 4. Holidays.]   I. Title. II. Series.
BP186.4 .M36   2002
297.3'62—dc21

                                                    2001002684

Do you celebrate Ramadan (RAHM-i-dahn)?

Ramadan is a holiday for Muslim (MUHZ-luhm) people. Muslims live in countries all over the world.

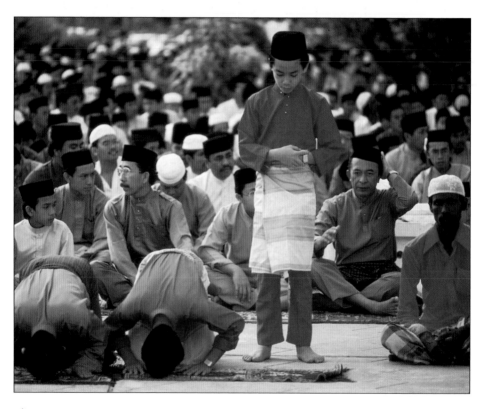

They follow a religion
called Islam (ISS-luhm).

June 2014

Sunday	Monday	Tuesday	Wednesday	Thursday	Friday	Saturday
1	2	3	4	5	6	7
8	9	10	11	12	13	14
15	16	17	18	19	20	21
22	23	24	25	26	27	28
Ramadan 29 Begins	30					

Ramadan lasts for a whole month. In fact, Ramadan *is* a month for Muslim people.

July 2014

Sunday	Monday	Tuesday	Wednesday	Thursday	Friday	Saturday
		1	2	3	4	5
6	7	8	9	10	11	12
13	14	15	16	17	18	19
20	21	22	23	24	25	26
Ramadan 27 Ends	28	29	30	31		

On the Muslim calendar, the ninth month is called Ramadan.

Ramadan is a special time
for Muslims. It is a time
for prayers.

Many Muslims pray five
times a day.

This Muslim family is saying prayers in their home.

These people are saying
prayers in a mosque (MOSK).

A mosque is a Muslim temple.

Ramadan is a time for friendship.

Some people travel a long way to be with their friends and family.

Ramadan is also a time for thinking. People think about how good their lives are. They think of ways to help people who are sick, poor, or hungry.

Many Muslims fast every day during Ramadan. When people fast, they do not eat.

Muslims do not eat or drink from the time the Sun rises to the time the Sun sets each day.

Families wake up before the Sun rises. They eat a big breakfast to get them through the day.

After sunset, they gather
for a big supper.

Not everyone fasts during Ramadan. Very old people, young children, and sick people usually do not fast.

Fasting all day is not easy. Part of Ramadan is making promises to yourself.

Do you think you could promise to fast?

Some children might
promise to try harder
at school.

Others might promise
to get along with their
brothers and sisters.

When the fast ends, Muslims have a three-day celebration.

People wear new clothes. They give gifts, pray, and eat a big feast.

Best of all, they enjoy being with their family and friends.

Words You Know

fast

celebration

friendship